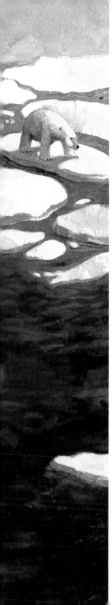

For my parents Lyn and Erich

Many thanks to the staff and children at
Flamingo Montessori Day Nursery, Burnham, Berkshire
and Teeny Boppers Nursery, Slough, Berkshire
for their help and advice.

Copyright © 1998 Zero to Ten Ltd
Illustrations copyright © 1996 Paul Hess

Edited by Anna McQuinn and Ambreen Husain, designed by Sarah Godwin and Suzy McGrath

While every effort has been made to trace the present copyright holders
we apologise in advance for any unintentional omission or error and will
be pleased to insert the appropriate acknowledgment in any subsequent edition.
Grateful acknowledgment is made to the following for permission to reprint the material listed below:
Seal from Laughing Time: Nonsense Poems by William J. Smith, copyright © 1953 William Jay Smith.
The Arctic Hare and **Fox** by Zarina Husain, copyright © 1998 Zero to Ten Ltd.
Penguins copyright © 1996 Miles Gibson, by kind permission of Jonathan Clowes Ltd, London.
Reindeer Express copyright © 1996 Gail Kredenser Mack.
The Walrus and **The Owl** copyright © 1983 by Jack Prelutsky, from Zoo Doings, 1983,
reprinted by permission of Greenwillow Books (a division of William Morrow & Company, Inc.).
Polar Bear from The ABC of Bumptious Beasts by Gail Kredenser, copyright © 1966 Gail Kredenser,
reprinted by permission of Gail Kredenser Mack.

First published in Great Britain in 1996 by De Agostini Editions.
First paperback edition published in 1998 by Zero to Ten Ltd., 46 Chalvey Road East Slough, Berkshire, SL1 2LR.

A CIP catalogue record for this book is available from the British Library.

ISBN 1-84089 041-X

Printed and bound in Spain.

Polar Animals

Illustrated by

PAUL HESS

Seal

SEE how he swims
With a swerve and a twist,
A flip of the flipper,
A flick of the wrist!

Arctic Hare

THE ARCTIC HARE in winter is white
To help him keep well out of sight.
In summer he's brown for the very same reason,
He changes his colour to suit the season.

Penguin

PENGUINS look immensely smart
It needs no explanation
They're simply waiting patiently
For a dinner invitation.

Reindeer

A WHISPERY GALLOP of hooves in the snow,
As reindeer play tag through each drift;
Splish-splush! Through the mush-slushy puddles they go –
O reindeer! Run silent, run swift!

Arctic Fox

LONE FOX, sly fox
prowling through the night,
silent as a shadow
under the full moon's light.

Walrus

THE thundery, blundery walrus
has a rubbery, blubbery hide.
He puffs up his neck when it's bedtime
and floats fast asleep on the tide.

Snowy Owl

THE OWL IS WARY, the owl is wise.
He knows all the names of the stars in the skies.
He hoots and toots and he lives by his wits,
but mostly he sits... and he sits... and he sits.

Polar Bear

THE secret of the polar bear
Is that he wears long underwear.